MW00931598

ISBN: 9798450102528
THATSSOANDREW.COM

property of a hoe named

let us begin with a how to...

NAME: ONLY IF YOU REMEMBER
DATE: MONTH AND YEAR... I LIKE TO ADD MY AGE FOR A FUN LITTLE TWIST
THEIR AGE: YES IT'S IMPORTANT TO KEEP UP WITH YOUR KINKS AND TASTE
LOCATION: ADDYS NOT NEEDED BUT LETS AT LEAST GET THE STATE & COUNTRY
RATINGS: NO HALF STARS! NO LIES!
WOULD U FUCK AGAIN? IT'S A SIMPLE YES/NO QUESTION...
HOW FAR? IF A HOLE WAS USED... IT COUNTS FOR THE BOOK! PERIODT.
NOTES: WHATEVER YOU FEEL YOU NEED TO PUT HERE... IT'S UP TO YOU.

remember, your body count literally doesn't matter and this isn't for anyone but yourself!

the v card robber

NAME:

DATE:

THEIR AGE:

LOCATION:

RATING: ☆☆☆☆☆

WOULD U FUCK AGAIN?

HOW FAR? (CHECK ALL THAT APPLY)

☐ HJ ☐ BJ ☐ THEY HIT IT

NOTES:

_____
_____
_____
_____
_____
_____
_____
_____
_____
_____
_____
_____
_____

the second
(hope it was better)

NAME:

DATE:

THEIR AGE:

LOCATION:

RATING: ☆☆☆☆☆

WOULD U FUCK AGAIN?

HOW FAR? (CHECK ALL THAT APPLY)

☐ HJ ☐ BJ ☐ THEY HIT IT

NOTES:

_____
_____
_____
_____
_____
_____
_____
_____
_____
_____
_____
_____
_____

the third

NAME:

DATE:

THEIR AGE:

LOCATION:

RATING: ☆☆☆☆☆

WOULD U FUCK AGAIN?

HOW FAR? (CHECK ALL THAT APPLY)

☐ HJ ☐ BJ ☐ THEY HIT IT

NOTES:

_____
_____
_____
_____
_____
_____
_____
_____
_____
_____
_____
_____

the fourth

NAME:

DATE:

THEIR AGE:

LOCATION:

RATING: ☆☆☆☆☆

WOULD U FUCK AGAIN?

HOW FAR? (CHECK ALL THAT APPLY)

☐ HJ ☐ BJ ☐ THEY HIT IT

NOTES:

_____

_____

_____

_____

_____

_____

_____

_____

_____

_____

_____

the fifth

NAME:

DATE:

THEIR AGE:

LOCATION:

RATING: ☆☆☆☆☆

WOULD U FUCK AGAIN?

HOW FAR? (CHECK ALL THAT APPLY)

☐ HJ ☐ BJ ☐ THEY HIT IT

NOTES:

_____
_____
_____
_____
_____
_____
_____
_____
_____
_____
_____

the sixth

NAME:

DATE:

THEIR AGE:

LOCATION:

RATING: ☆☆☆☆☆

WOULD U FUCK AGAIN?

HOW FAR? (CHECK ALL THAT APPLY)

⬜ HJ ⬜ BJ ⬜ THEY HIT IT

NOTES:

_____
_____
_____
_____
_____
_____
_____
_____
_____
_____
_____
_____

the seventh

NAME:

DATE:

THEIR AGE:

LOCATION:

RATING: ☆☆☆☆☆

WOULD U FUCK AGAIN?

HOW FAR? (CHECK ALL THAT APPLY)

☐ HJ ☐ BJ ☐ THEY HIT IT

NOTES:

_____
_____
_____
_____
_____
_____
_____
_____
_____
_____
_____
_____
_____

the eighth

NAME:

DATE:

THEIR AGE:

LOCATION:

RATING: ☆☆☆☆☆

WOULD U FUCK AGAIN?

HOW FAR? (CHECK ALL THAT APPLY)

☐ HJ ☐ BJ ☐ THEY HIT IT

NOTES:

_____
_____
_____
_____
_____
_____
_____
_____
_____
_____
_____
_____
_____

the ninth

NAME:

DATE:

THEIR AGE:

LOCATION:

RATING: ☆☆☆☆☆

WOULD U FUCK AGAIN?

HOW FAR? (CHECK ALL THAT APPLY)

☐ HJ ☐ BJ ☐ THEY HIT IT

NOTES:

_____
_____
_____
_____
_____
_____
_____
_____
_____
_____
_____
_____

the tenth

NAME:

DATE:

THEIR AGE:

LOCATION:

RATING: ☆☆☆☆☆

WOULD U FUCK AGAIN?

HOW FAR? (CHECK ALL THAT APPLY)

☐ HJ ☐ BJ ☐ THEY HIT IT

NOTES:

_____
_____
_____
_____
_____
_____
_____
_____
_____
_____
_____

ps... we are done counting now

eleven in heaven

NAME:

DATE:

THEIR AGE:

LOCATION:

RATING: ☆☆☆☆☆

WOULD U FUCK AGAIN?

HOW FAR? (CHECK ALL THAT APPLY)

☐ HJ ☐ BJ ☐ THEY HIT IT

NOTES:

_____
_____
_____
_____
_____
_____
_____
_____
_____
_____
_____
_____
_____

numbers don't matter

NAME:

DATE:

THEIR AGE:

LOCATION:

RATING: ☆☆☆☆☆

WOULD U FUCK AGAIN?

HOW FAR? (CHECK ALL THAT APPLY)

☐ HJ ☐ BJ ☐ THEY HIT IT

NOTES:

_____

_____

_____

_____

_____

_____

_____

_____

_____

_____

_____

_____

_____

NAME:

DATE:

THEIR AGE:

LOCATION:

RATING: ☆☆☆☆☆

WOULD U FUCK AGAIN?

HOW FAR? (CHECK ALL THAT APPLY)

☐ HJ ☐ BJ ☐ THEY HIT IT

NOTES:

_____
_____
_____
_____
_____
_____
_____
_____
_____
_____
_____
_____

you're doing amazing sweetie

NAME:

DATE:

THEIR AGE:

LOCATION:

RATING: ☆☆☆☆☆

WOULD U FUCK AGAIN?

HOW FAR? (CHECK ALL THAT APPLY)

☐ **HJ** ☐ **BJ** ☐ **THEY HIT IT**

NOTES:

_____
_____
_____
_____
_____
_____
_____
_____
_____
_____
_____
_____

get em!

NAME:

DATE:

THEIR AGE:

LOCATION:

RATING: ☆☆☆☆☆

WOULD U FUCK AGAIN?

HOW FAR? (CHECK ALL THAT APPLY)

☐ HJ ☐ BJ ☐ THEY HIT IT

NOTES:

_____
_____
_____
_____
_____
_____
_____
_____
_____
_____
_____
_____

that is so fetch

NAME:

DATE:

THEIR AGE:

LOCATION:

RATING: ☆☆☆☆☆

WOULD U FUCK AGAIN?

HOW FAR? (CHECK ALL THAT APPLY)

☐ HJ ☐ BJ ☐ THEY HIT IT

NOTES:

_____
_____
_____
_____
_____
_____
_____
_____
_____
_____
_____
_____

just keep swimming

NAME:

DATE:

THEIR AGE:

LOCATION:

RATING: ☆☆☆☆☆

WOULD U FUCK AGAIN?

HOW FAR? (CHECK ALL THAT APPLY)

☐ HJ ☐ BJ ☐ THEY HIT IT

NOTES:

_____
_____
_____
_____
_____
_____
_____
_____
_____
_____
_____
_____
_____
_____

NAME:

DATE:

THEIR AGE:

LOCATION:

RATING: ☆☆☆☆☆

WOULD U FUCK AGAIN?

HOW FAR? (CHECK ALL THAT APPLY)

☐ HJ ☐ BJ ☐ THEY HIT IT

NOTES:

_____

_____

_____

_____

_____

_____

_____

_____

_____

_____

_____

_____

NAME:

DATE:

THEIR AGE:

LOCATION:

RATING: ☆☆☆☆☆

WOULD U FUCK AGAIN?

HOW FAR? (CHECK ALL THAT APPLY)

☐ HJ ☐ BJ ☐ THEY HIT IT

NOTES:

_____
_____
_____
_____
_____
_____
_____
_____
_____
_____
_____
_____
_____

after twenty it really does not matter

NAME:

DATE:

THEIR AGE:

LOCATION:

RATING: ☆☆☆☆☆

WOULD U FUCK AGAIN?

HOW FAR? (CHECK ALL THAT APPLY)

☐ HJ ☐ BJ ☐ THEY HIT IT

NOTES:

_____
_____
_____
_____
_____
_____
_____
_____
_____
_____
_____
_____

ooh baby we hit the twenties

NAME:

DATE:

THEIR AGE:

LOCATION:

RATING: ☆☆☆☆☆

WOULD U FUCK AGAIN?

HOW FAR? (CHECK ALL THAT APPLY)

☐ HJ ☐ BJ ☐ THEY HIT IT

NOTES:

_____
_____
_____
_____
_____
_____
_____
_____
_____
_____
_____
_____
_____

NAME:

DATE:

THEIR AGE:

LOCATION:

RATING: ☆☆☆☆☆

WOULD U FUCK AGAIN?

HOW FAR? (CHECK ALL THAT APPLY)

☐ HJ ☐ BJ ☐ THEY HIT IT

NOTES:

_____

_____

_____

_____

_____

_____

_____

_____

_____

_____

_____

_____

NAME:

DATE:

THEIR AGE:

LOCATION:

RATING: ☆☆☆☆☆

WOULD U FUCK AGAIN?

HOW FAR? (CHECK ALL THAT APPLY)

☐ HJ ☐ BJ ☐ THEY HIT IT

NOTES:

_____
_____
_____
_____
_____
_____
_____
_____
_____
_____
_____
_____

what's better than 24?

NAME:

DATE:

THEIR AGE:

LOCATION:

RATING: ☆☆☆☆☆

WOULD U FUCK AGAIN?

HOW FAR? (CHECK ALL THAT APPLY)

☐ HJ ☐ BJ ☐ THEY HIT IT

NOTES:

_____
_____
_____
_____
_____
_____
_____
_____
_____
_____
_____
_____

twenty five duh

NAME:

DATE:

THEIR AGE:

LOCATION:

RATING: ☆☆☆☆☆

WOULD U FUCK AGAIN?

HOW FAR? (CHECK ALL THAT APPLY)

☐ HJ ☐ BJ ☐ THEY HIT IT

NOTES:

_____
_____
_____
_____
_____
_____
_____
_____
_____
_____
_____
_____

NAME:

DATE:

THEIR AGE:

LOCATION:

RATING: ☆☆☆☆☆

WOULD U FUCK AGAIN?

HOW FAR? (CHECK ALL THAT APPLY)

☐ HJ ☐ BJ ☐ THEY HIT IT

NOTES:

_____

_____

_____

_____

_____

_____

_____

_____

_____

_____

_____

_____

NAME:

DATE:

THEIR AGE:

LOCATION:

RATING: ☆☆☆☆☆

WOULD U FUCK AGAIN?

HOW FAR? (CHECK ALL THAT APPLY)

☐ HJ ☐ BJ ☐ THEY HIT IT

NOTES:

_____

_____

_____

_____

_____

_____

_____

_____

_____

_____

_____

_____

NAME:

DATE:

THEIR AGE:

LOCATION:

RATING: ☆☆☆☆☆

WOULD U FUCK AGAIN?

HOW FAR? (CHECK ALL THAT APPLY)

☐ HJ ☐ BJ ☐ THEY HIT IT

NOTES:

_____

_____

_____

_____

_____

_____

_____

_____

_____

_____

_____

_____

ooh baby you are on a roll

NAME:

DATE:

THEIR AGE:

LOCATION:

RATING: ☆☆☆☆☆

WOULD U FUCK AGAIN?

HOW FAR? (CHECK ALL THAT APPLY)

☐ HJ ☐ BJ ☐ THEY HIT IT

NOTES:

_____
_____
_____
_____
_____
_____
_____
_____
_____
_____
_____
_____
_____

NAME:

DATE:

THEIR AGE:

LOCATION:

RATING: ☆☆☆☆☆

WOULD U FUCK AGAIN?

HOW FAR? (CHECK ALL THAT APPLY)

☐ HJ ☐ BJ ☐ THEY HIT IT

NOTES:

_____

_____

_____

_____

_____

_____

_____

_____

_____

_____

_____

_____

NAME:

DATE:

THEIR AGE:

LOCATION:

RATING: ☆☆☆☆☆

WOULD U FUCK AGAIN?

HOW FAR? (CHECK ALL THAT APPLY)

☐ HJ ☐ BJ ☐ THEY HIT IT

NOTES:

_____

_____

_____

_____

_____

_____

_____

_____

_____

_____

_____

_____

you. are. killing. it.

NAME:

DATE:

THEIR AGE:

LOCATION:

RATING: ☆☆☆☆☆

WOULD U FUCK AGAIN?

HOW FAR? (CHECK ALL THAT APPLY)

☐ HJ ☐ BJ ☐ THEY HIT IT

NOTES:

_____
_____
_____
_____
_____
_____
_____
_____
_____
_____
_____
_____

NAME:

DATE:

THEIR AGE:

LOCATION:

RATING: ☆☆☆☆☆

WOULD U FUCK AGAIN?

HOW FAR? (CHECK ALL THAT APPLY)

☐ HJ ☐ BJ ☐ THEY HIT IT

NOTES:

_____

_____

_____

_____

_____

_____

_____

_____

_____

_____

_____

_____

_____

NAME:

DATE:

THEIR AGE:

LOCATION:

RATING: ☆☆☆☆☆

WOULD U FUCK AGAIN?

HOW FAR? (CHECK ALL THAT APPLY)

☐ HJ ☐ BJ ☐ THEY HIT IT

NOTES:

_____
_____
_____
_____
_____
_____
_____
_____
_____
_____
_____
_____

NAME:

DATE:

THEIR AGE:

LOCATION:

RATING: ☆☆☆☆☆

WOULD U FUCK AGAIN?

HOW FAR? (CHECK ALL THAT APPLY)

☐ HJ ☐ BJ ☐ THEY HIT IT

NOTES:

_____

_____

_____

_____

_____

_____

_____

_____

_____

_____

_____

_____

NAME:

DATE:

THEIR AGE:

LOCATION:

RATING: ☆☆☆☆☆

WOULD U FUCK AGAIN?

HOW FAR? (CHECK ALL THAT APPLY)

☐ HJ ☐ BJ ☐ THEY HIT IT

NOTES:

_____

_____

_____

_____

_____

_____

_____

_____

_____

_____

_____

_____

does anyone get 5 stars anymore?

NAME:

DATE:

THEIR AGE:

LOCATION:

RATING: ☆☆☆☆☆

WOULD U FUCK AGAIN?

HOW FAR? (CHECK ALL THAT APPLY)

☐ HJ ☐ BJ ☐ THEY HIT IT

NOTES:

_____

_____

_____

_____

_____

_____

_____

_____

_____

_____

_____

_____

_____

NAME:

DATE:

THEIR AGE:

LOCATION:

RATING: ☆☆☆☆☆

WOULD U FUCK AGAIN?

HOW FAR? (CHECK ALL THAT APPLY)

☐ HJ ☐ BJ ☐ THEY HIT IT

NOTES:

_____
_____
_____
_____
_____
_____
_____
_____
_____
_____
_____

NAME:

DATE:

THEIR AGE:

LOCATION:

RATING: ☆☆☆☆☆

WOULD U FUCK AGAIN?

HOW FAR? (CHECK ALL THAT APPLY)

☐ HJ ☐ BJ ☐ THEY HIT IT

NOTES:

_____
_____
_____
_____
_____
_____
_____
_____
_____
_____
_____
_____

NAME:

DATE:

THEIR AGE:

LOCATION:

RATING: ☆☆☆☆☆

WOULD U FUCK AGAIN?

HOW FAR? (CHECK ALL THAT APPLY)

☐ HJ ☐ BJ ☐ THEY HIT IT

NOTES:

_____
_____
_____
_____
_____
_____
_____
_____
_____
_____
_____
_____
_____

NAME:

DATE:

THEIR AGE:

LOCATION:

RATING: ☆☆☆☆☆

WOULD U FUCK AGAIN?

HOW FAR? (CHECK ALL THAT APPLY)

☐ HJ ☐ BJ ☐ THEY HIT IT

NOTES:

_____

_____

_____

_____

_____

_____

_____

_____

_____

_____

_____

_____

NAME:

DATE:

THEIR AGE:

LOCATION:

RATING: ☆☆☆☆☆

WOULD U FUCK AGAIN?

HOW FAR? (CHECK ALL THAT APPLY)

☐ HJ ☐ BJ ☐ THEY HIT IT

NOTES:

_____
_____
_____
_____
_____
_____
_____
_____
_____
_____
_____
_____

NAME:

DATE:

THEIR AGE:

LOCATION:

RATING: ☆☆☆☆☆

WOULD U FUCK AGAIN?

HOW FAR? (CHECK ALL THAT APPLY)

☐ HJ ☐ BJ ☐ THEY HIT IT

NOTES:

_____

_____

_____

_____

_____

_____

_____

_____

_____

_____

_____

NAME:

DATE:

THEIR AGE:

LOCATION:

RATING: ☆☆☆☆☆

WOULD U FUCK AGAIN?

HOW FAR? (CHECK ALL THAT APPLY)

☐ HJ ☐ BJ ☐ THEY HIT IT

NOTES:

_____
_____
_____
_____
_____
_____
_____
_____
_____
_____
_____
_____

NAME:

DATE:

THEIR AGE:

LOCATION:

RATING: ☆☆☆☆☆

WOULD U FUCK AGAIN?

HOW FAR? (CHECK ALL THAT APPLY)

☐ HJ ☐ BJ ☐ THEY HIT IT

NOTES:

_____
_____
_____
_____
_____
_____
_____
_____
_____
_____
_____
_____

NAME:

DATE:

THEIR AGE:

LOCATION:

RATING: ☆☆☆☆☆

WOULD U FUCK AGAIN?

HOW FAR? (CHECK ALL THAT APPLY)

☐ HJ ☐ BJ ☐ THEY HIT IT

NOTES:

_____
_____
_____
_____
_____
_____
_____
_____
_____
_____
_____
_____

NAME:

DATE:

THEIR AGE:

LOCATION:

RATING: ☆☆☆☆☆

WOULD U FUCK AGAIN?

HOW FAR? (CHECK ALL THAT APPLY)

☐ HJ ☐ BJ ☐ THEY HIT IT

NOTES:

_____
_____
_____
_____
_____
_____
_____
_____
_____
_____
_____
_____

48 is a great number

NAME:

DATE:

THEIR AGE:

LOCATION:

RATING: ☆☆☆☆☆

WOULD U FUCK AGAIN?

HOW FAR? (CHECK ALL THAT APPLY)

☐ HJ ☐ BJ ☐ THEY HIT IT

NOTES:

_____

_____

_____

_____

_____

_____

_____

_____

_____

_____

_____

_____

this journal is officially

FILLED

*so flip back through and tell me...
who was the most memberable?*

now go fuck them one more time :)